WATERLOO LOCAL SCHOOL
Middle School Library Title II

EARL THE PEARL

The Story of Earl Monroe

by Robert B. Jackson

illustrated with photographs

New York　　　　Henry Z. Walck, Inc.

Copyright © 1969, 1971 by Robert B. Jackson
All rights reserved
Revised edition 1971
ISBN: 0-8098-2064-1 (hardcover)
ISBN: 0-8098-2905-3 (paperback)
Library of Congress Catalog Card Number: 75-174748
Printed in the United States of America

Special thanks are due Laurence J. Weber, Director of Public Information, Winston-Salem State College, Winston-Salem, N.C., for his help in the preparation of this book. The picture on page 17 is reproduced with his permission, while those on pages 14 and 31 are reprinted through the courtesy of the Baltimore Bullets. United Press International supplied the photographs on pages 10, 28, 33, 39, 42, 53, 61 and 63, while those on pages 21, 22, 44 and 51 are from Wide World Photos, Inc.

CONTENTS

1. *"Earl, Earl! Earl the Pearl!"* 9

2. *Unpolished Pearl,* 12

3. *Rookie of the Year,* 24

4. *Storybook Season,* 35

5. *Playoff Upset,* 48

6. *"Best in the World?"* 60

1
"EARL, EARL! EARL THE PEARL!"

THE NEW YORK Knickerbocker was pressing closely as they came downcourt, and Baltimore's Earl Monroe quickly dribbled the ball—first with his right hand, then with his left, then between his legs and behind his back—to prevent the possibility of a steal. Turning his back and using his body as a shield in the forecourt, he continued his advance, then suddenly passed off to a teammate and cut toward the basket. Eluding another defender, he took a return pass and began his drive, now dribbling at top speed.

The opposing Knick went up with him as he took his shot, and Earl seemed to pause for a frac-

CLOSELY FOLLOWED BY NEW YORK'S WALT FRAZIER, EARL CUTS TOWARD THE BASKET. NOTE THE HAND-PLAY OF BOTH.

tion of a second at the top of his leap, moving flashily in one direction before shooting from another. Confused by the fake, the New York player was completely out of position as the ball rolled through the hoop, putting the Bullets ahead once more. And even as Earl was in midair, that familiar chant was already resounding in Baltimore's Civic Center, "Earl, Earl! Earl the Pearl! Earl, Earl, Best in the World!"

2
UNPOLISHED PEARL

MOST GUIDEBOOKS mention that Philadelphia is the fourth-largest city in the United States as well as the second-largest port, then stress the city's strong cultural tradition and its important place in the early history of this country. Not always added is the fact that there are extensive Negro ghetto areas in Philadelphia, located in what have been called some of the worst slums in the world.

Recent civic development programs are attempting to improve this situation, but such plans did not exist when Vernon Earl Monroe, born November 21, 1944, was growing up in the South Philadelphia slums. His parents ran a grocery store there; and

Earl has said the Monroes were relatively well-off in comparison to the other people in the neighborhood. Even so, the poverty, crime and dreary hopelessness—not to mention the segregation—of the ghetto made a strong impression on him as a young boy.

Despite this background, Earl has recalled that his first ambition in life was to be a comedian. His primary interest in grade school was soccer, however, and he was good enough at it to be chosen an all-city halfback. Surprisingly enough, he was not much of a basketball player at this age. Now six feet, three and a half inches tall and weighing one hundred and ninety pounds, Earl was short and somewhat overweight as a youngster. Also, as he now remembers, he did not have his jump shot yet, and as a result was seldom chosen to play in the neighborhood games.

"You feel it when you're not picked in those games," he recently told a reporter. Then, when he was about fourteen, a series of events occurred that made him popular on the courts of the South Philly playgrounds and started him toward his present National Basketball Association career as well.

First of all, an injury to an ankle stopped him

ALTHOUGH SHORT AND OVERWEIGHT AS A BOY, EARL IS NOW SIX FEET THREE AND ONE-HALF INCHES TALL AND WEIGHS ONE HUNDRED AND NINETY POUNDS.

from playing soccer. And at about the same time he began to grow rapidly, suddenly springing up to a trim six feet. Most important of all, perhaps because of being left out of those pickup games,

Earl began to practice his shooting and ball control for long periods of time.

Summers are hot and humid in Philadelphia, but Earl was out on the playgrounds ten hours a day as soon as school was over, improving the accuracy of his shots, developing new ones, and tirelessly practicing his dribbling. He remembers coming home at night with his shoulders aching, and he was later to have problems with his knees because of so much running up and down on macadam and concrete courts; but his basketball skills were maturing rapidly.

"That's where you learn how to really play the game," Earl once remarked. "I'd chip in a quarter for gas every day just to ride ten miles to a court and then hope they didn't have enough guys when they chose up sides so I could get in." Some of the "guys" he played against as a teenager were other NBA stars of the future such as Guy Rodgers, Wally Jones and Wilt Chamberlain.

Still, he did not make the John Bartram High School team until halfway through the season of his junior year. By the time he was a senior he had earned a statewide reputation, however; and one magazine has reported that even established NBA players were dropping by to see Earl in action that winter. At this stage of his career he was a center averaging twenty-one points a game.

His concentration on improving his court performance caused his grades to suffer, and Earl graduated from John Bartram in the lower half of his class. Recruiters from several colleges with strong basketball teams were naturally interested in him; but Earl decided to attend Temple Prep in Philadelphia for a year instead of going to college immediately, hoping to meet the entrance requirements for Temple University, also located in Philadelphia.

Becoming discouraged with his progress before the end of the first semester, he dropped out to take a job as a shipping clerk in a knitting mill. His salary was less than sixty dollars a week, and he has since been quoted as saying, "It didn't take me long to realize that working so hard for so little was definitely not my bag."

At the time Earl graduated from high school, a friend had tried to interest him in Winston-Salem State College, a mostly Negro college in North Carolina. The friend continued his recruiting efforts while Earl was working in the factory; and after he had given up his job, Earl decided to enroll there.

Winston-Salem is a small college located in the heart of tobacco country specializing in teacher and nursing education. Nearly all of its fourteen hundred students come from North Carolina, and over two-thirds are girls. Nevertheless, the Winston-Salem Rams are members of a tough (if little-reported)

EARL (RIGHT) APPEARED IN MANY STUDENT SHOWS AT WINSTON-SALEM, NEARLY ALWAYS AS PART OF A COMEDY ROUTINE.

basketball conference, the Central Intercollegiate Athletic Association; and in 1967 Winston-Salem became the first Negro school—as well as the first Southern college, black *or* white—to win the National Collegiate Athletic Association's College Division championship.

The most important reason for Winston-Salem's basketball success has been its coach, Clarence E. Gaines, who is often called "Big House" Gaines because of his large size. Through Earl's senior year Gaines-coached teams had won 415 games while losing only 153; and Earl has said that it was Coach Gaines who did the most to make him the player he is today. As the local newspapers liked to put it, what brought Earl down to Winston-Salem was "grits, gravy and Gaines."

Coach Gaines, known for his tough discipline as well as his teaching ability, converted Earl from a center into a shooting guard and helped him polish his offensive skills further. The sixth man as a freshman, Earl averaged only 7.1 points a game; but by the end of his junior year he averaged 29.8 points a game and ranked eleventh in the NCAA College Division for scoring. The Ram record that season was twenty-one games won and five lost.

He improved further as a senior, and, while not as well-known nationally as such widely publicized University Division stars as Lew Alcindor or Jimmy Walker, Earl was closely scouted by the pros. One NBA coach has been quoted as calling him "the only college player in the last fifteen years that I'd pay to see play again, and that includes Bill Bradley, Jim Walker and Lew Alcindor." Playing in thirty-two games Earl ran up a total of 1,329 points, an all-time collegiate record, and an average of 41.5, highest in both NCAA divisions. His single-game high, also best in the country, was a blistering sixty-eight points, scored against Fayetteville State.

Mildly superstitious, Earl decided not to have his socks washed after the high-scoring Fayetteville game. Two nights later, against a stronger team, he hit for fifty-eight points, making twenty-two of twenty-four field goals attempted and fourteen of sixteen foul shots in a truly sensational performance. When his total dropped to thirty points in the next game, however, he sent the socks to the laundry. Clean-shod next time out, he scored his usual forty.

Earl even made fifty-three points during a game in which he had badly sprained a wrist early in the first half; and against Johnson C. Smith University he completed twenty-five of twenty-six free throws, the best single free-throw performance in the division that season. While he was at Winston-Salem, a local newspaper once ran a series of such statistics under the headline, "These are Earl's Pearls," and the name has been with him ever since.

During Earl's senior year the only game the Rams lost was to North Carolina Agricultural and Technical State University on a night when he had a rare lapse of form. (The North Carolina A & T player covering him was a boy who had grown up playing one-on-one with Earl on the playgrounds of South Philadelphia.) As its co-captain and leading scorer, Earl led the team to a thirty-one and one season; and, in a post-season tournament, to the championship of the NCAA's College Division.

In NCAA championship play the 1967 Rams had successive victories over Baldwin-Wallace, Akron and Long Island University; then beat Kentucky Wesleyan, known for winning the championship in other years, in the semifinals. Against Southwest Missouri in the final game, a 77–74 squeaker, Earl made sixteen field goals and sank eight free throws for a total of forty points, more than half of Winston-Salem's total. He scored nineteen points

AS A SENIOR AT WINSTON-SALEM, EARL SET A NEW COLLEGIATE SCORING RECORD AND LED THE RAMS TO AN NCAA COLLEGE DIVISION CHAMPIONSHIP.

SCORING TWENTY-NINE POINTS IN THE L.I.U. GAME OF THE 1967 NCAA COLLEGE DIVISION TOURNAMENT, EARL BROUGHT HIS SEASON'S SCORING TOTAL TO 1,265 POINTS, AN ALL-TIME RECORD. HE FURTHER INCREASED HIS RECORD TO 1,329 IN LATER GAMES OF THE SERIES.

in the last nine minutes alone, including the basket that tied the score for the last time, and two foul shots with twenty-five seconds left that put the game on ice.

He was elected Most Valuable Player of the tournament, NCAA College Division Player of the Year, and also to both United Press International and Associated Press's Small College All-American teams for 1967. Winston-Salem later retired uniform number ten, the number Earl usually still wears with the Bullets.

At the end of the season the National Association of Basketball Coaches named Coach Gaines College Division Coach of the Year. His comment to a local newspaperman was, "I know I'll never have a better season. Why? Because I know I'll never have another Earl Monroe."

3
ROOKIE OF THE YEAR

AT THE TIME Earl graduated from Winston-Salem, the recently organized American Basketball Association was trying to establish itself as a serious rival to the NBA. It has been reported that the ABA's Pittsburgh Pipers offered more money to Earl than he was later to accept from Baltimore; but he was anxious to match his skills against the superior competition of the NBA teams, and such NBA superstars as Wilt Chamberlain and Bill Russell.

In any event, Earl quickly signed a one-year contract with the Bullets for $19,000 before consulting with Coach Gaines, who had agreed to negotiate for him. The angered Gaines was later able to increase the terms to $20,000 a year for two years, but even under these conditions it was a real bargain for Baltimore.

Earl, who had played on a winning team in college, was to spend his first season as a professional with a club that had a history of losing. The original Baltimore Bullets, members of an eastern weekend league, had been taken into the Basketball Association of America in 1947. (The following season the BAA merged with the National League to become today's NBA.) While the Bullets promptly won the league championship that first year, they slipped badly from then on. In both the seasons of 1952–53 and 1953–54 they won only sixteen games all schedule long; and the team was finally given up as hopeless and disbanded in the fall of 1954 after winning only three of fourteen contests.

It was nine years before big-league basketball returned to Baltimore, and then not with the brightest of hopes. In 1961 the NBA had awarded a franchise for a new team in Chicago, called the Packers because they played in an auditorium near the stockyards. The Packers were not only unsuccessful on the floor (eighteen won and sixty-two lost), they were losers at the box office as well; and their owners arranged to move the team to Baltimore. Because it would be a year before the new Civic

Center would be ready for them in Baltimore, the Packers played the 1962-63 season in Chicago. Despite two new coaches, a different building and even a new name—the Chicago Zephyrs—they finished dead last in their division once more.

Playing in Baltimore in 1963-64, the ex-Packers/Zephyrs were renamed the Bullets after the earlier team there and finished fourth in the Western Division. This represented an improvement from last place to next-to-last; and the following year they moved up to third, making the playoffs for the championship but losing in the divisional finals.

In 1965-66 the Bullets managed a most encouraging second-place finish, then lost their first three playoff games in a row to St. Louis and were quickly eliminated from championship competition. In 1966-67, the season before Earl joined Baltimore, Chicago returned to the Western Division, and the Bullets were moved into the tougher Eastern Division where they fared dismally. Under a parade of three different coaches they won only twenty games while losing sixty-one, a percentage of .247 and the worst record in the league.

In the annual spring draft of college basketball players, NBA clubs make their choices in reverse order of final league standings to keep the teams as evenly matched as possible. In 1967 this meant that Baltimore and Detroit, last-place finishers in the East and West respectively, flipped a coin for first pick.

Bullet Coach Gene Shue's first choice was to have been Jimmy Walker of Providence College, except that Baltimore lost the toss. Detroit took Walker instead, and Shue had to come up with another selection.

The first time Shue had seen Earl play was the North Carolina A & T game, the only game Winston-Salem lost that season, and Earl had not been at his best. "He had an awful night. Frankly, I wanted no part of him," Shue later told a reporter.

But the Baltimore coach later saw Earl star in the tryouts for the 1967 Pan-American Games and quickly changed his mind. He now calls Earl "the most exciting player in basketball." Even so, some say that Baltimore officials once struggled through a twelve-hour debate before finally deciding to make Earl their number-one choice.

Earl made his professional debut in Baltimore on October 18, 1967, against the New York Knickerbockers in the season's opener. While he had not scored much in preseason exhibition games, he had wisely used the time to learn his teammates' moves and the NBA style of play instead. Putting this knowledge to use against the Knicks, he shot for twenty-two points, had five assists, and immediately established himself as a particular favorite of the crowd with his unique shooting and dashing ball control.

News of Earl's fancy moves and colorful manner

BALTIMORE DRAFTED EARL ON MAY 3, 1967. CELEBRATING THE OCCASION ARE ARNOLD HEFT, THEN A CO-OWNER OF THE BULLETS, COACH GENE SHUE, EARL AND THE PRESENT OWNER, ABE POLLIN.

spread rapidly among the basketball fans of Baltimore, and ticket sales for the second game of the season set a new record for the Bullets. The large crowd was not disappointed as Earl hit for sixteen points, made five assists, and even got eight rebounds against no less a team than the Boston Celtics. Although powerful Boston won the game by outscoring the Bullets in the later stages, it was a close contest until the third quarter.

The fans were again delighted by Earl's glittering court behavior. He repeatedly dribbled flashily downcourt, turned his back on a defender, and then leaped over him with a spinning fallaway jump shot; and each time he did so, the crowd shouted "Earl the Pearl! Earl the Pearl!" once more.

The Bullets seemed so improved in these first two games that sportswriters and fans alike became unduly optimistic about Baltimore's chances for the rest of the season. In a feature article about Earl, unusual in itself since he had played only two games of professional ball at the time, *Sports Illustrated* even went so far as to predict "they can be the finest Baltimore team ever."

The Bullets did in fact win their next two games, but then suffered a disastrous losing streak, dropping eight games in a row. After winning five of their next eight, they lost another six straight, looking much like the inept Packers or Zephyrs of old. By the middle of December they were playing only .310 ball, and the optimism of October seemed badly misplaced.

Part of the problem was the lack of a big man who could get the ball from the defensive backboards and pitch out to the breaking shooters; but Baltimore's ball-hungry shooters were causing trouble in themselves. Each man was playing for himself alone; and there was so little Bullet team play for a time that one writer commented the only way Baltimore could win was to give each player a ball of his own.

A large factor in getting the Bullets to function as a team instead was Earl himself. In spite of being a rookie, he played in every game on the schedule, the leading Bullet (and tenth in the league) for total time played during 1967–68. His defensive play was weak at first (some coaches say this is still the Pearl's flaw), but his shooting and ball-handling became dazzling. And as he grew more familiar with his teammates and the other players in the league, he began to "quarterback" more and more, taking charge of the offense and setting up its plays.

EARL, SHOWN HERE PASSING BEHIND HIS BACK, ALWAYS DE-
LIGHTS THE FANS WITH HIS DASHING STYLE OF PLAY.

As the Bullets learned to play as a team instead of five individual stars, their won-lost record improved. At the time of the All-Star Game at mid-season they had been seventeen and thirty; during the second part of the year they won nineteen and lost sixteen.

But record books consider the season as a whole and show Baltimore as winning thirty-six and losing forty-six in 1967–68, a percentage of only .439. The Bullets finished last in the East again, three games behind fifth-place Cincinnati and twenty-six behind first-place Philadelphia.

Earl's personal record for the season was a brilliant one in contrast. He scored a total of 1,991 points over the eighty-two games for an average of 24.3 points per game, tying with Wilt Chamberlain for the third-highest point-average in the league. Also, he led Baltimore in games played, minutes played, field goals attempted, field goals made (.453), free throws attempted, field goals made (.781), and assists (4.2 per game). Of the last thirty-five games of the season, he was the Bullets' top scorer in twenty-five, and he set a new Baltimore record with his game-high effort of fifty-six points against the Los Angeles Lakers.

Second only to Wilt in most points scored in a

DURING A GAME AGAINST LOS ANGELES IN 1968, EARL WAS BOXED IN BY TWO LAKERS AND UNABLE TO COMPLETE THIS JUMP PASS. CHARACTERISTICALLY, HE REACTED INSTANTLY AND PASSED OVER HIS SHOULDER TO GUS JOHNSON (NO. 25) BEFORE HITTING THE FLOOR.

single game, he tied for second in the league in most free throws made in a single game (seventeen); and he was third in most field goals scored in one game (twenty) as well. Little wonder that in April of 1968 when the NBA Rookie of the Year was elected, seventy-eight of seventy-nine sports writers and broadcasters voted for Earl the Pearl.

4
STORYBOOK SEASON

A LAST-PLACE finish for the second season in a row was hardly what the Baltimore owners and fans had been dreaming of, but there was one consolation. The Bullets would again pick first in the spring draft of college players.

They lost the toss of the coin with the last-place Western club, just as they had the year before while drafting Earl; and once again the loss proved fortunate for Baltimore in the long run. The San Diego Rockets grabbed high-scoring Elvin Hayes of Houston, NCAA Player of the Year; and the Bullets decided on Wes Unseld, twice an All-American at the University of Louisville.

Even though Hayes led the NBA in scoring that season, Unseld soon demonstrated himself much the better choice for Baltimore. The Bullets were already well-stocked with effective shooters such as Gus Johnson, Kevin Loughery and Jack Marin—not to mention Earl, of course—their great lack being someone to get the ball for them. Unseld was not only able to fill that need, he quickly developed into one of the best defensive centers in the league and helped to turn the Bullets into a winning team at last.

He started the season as a forward, but was playing regularly in the pivot after only a dozen games or so. Thought at first to be too "small" at six seven to go up against the other big men in the NBA, Wes nevertheless showed great ability at winning the savage battle for defensive rebounds and whipping outlet passes to the fast-breaking shooters. He averaged 18.1 rebounds a game for the season; and at its conclusion the other NBA players showed their respect for his skills by voting him the Most Valuable Player in the league. The sports writers named him Rookie of the Year and, along with Earl, to the NBA All-Star team ahead of such supercenters as Wilt Chamberlain and Bill Russell.

With Unseld to get the ball, Earl to direct the floor play, and a Bullet bench jammed with sharpshooters, Baltimore finally had a team of championship ability. There was no more talk of moving the team still another time to Houston or Miami Beach; and internal matters on the club also improved when owner Abe Pollin bought out his two partners and revised the front-office organization, saying "The old Bullets are gone. This is a new era."

The 1968–69 season was a critical time for other teams in the Eastern Division as well. The seemingly endless domination of the Boston Celtics was increasingly subject to question in preseason forecasts, for one thing. The Celts had won the NBA championship ten of the past twelve years, eight of them in a row, but many experts thought that Bill Russell, the great Boston player-coach, and the rest of his team were finally slowing with age. Of course, much the same thing had been said early in the previous season, and Boston had proven the sportswriters wrong by finishing second, winning the divisional semifinals with Philadelphia after being down three games to one, and then going on to beat the Western champions, the Los Angeles Lakers, for still another NBA title.

In the offseason the Philadelphia 76'ers, Boston's arch-rivals in recent years and league champions in 1967, had traded their controversial center, Wilt Chamberlain, to the Lakers; and Philadelphia coach Alex Hannum had jumped to the ABA. Nevertheless, as the season opened the 76'ers were playing a fast hustling game under new coach Jack Ramsay and didn't seem to miss Wilt very much, after all.

Then there were the New York Knickerbockers. Although the Bullets had scornfully been called the Humpty-Dumptys of the NBA in past years, there were many fans in New York willing to claim the title for their own club. Nothing had ever gone very well for the Knicks, including their draft choices; and while there were predictions each year that they were finally about to do much better, somehow they never did.

Typically, in spite of excellent material and considerable improvement at the conclusion of the previous season, they got off to a horrible start in 1968, losing thirteen of their first nineteen games. Then, at that point, all the predictions began to come true at last. After an advantageous trade with the Detroit Pistons the Knicks suddenly jelled and became the terrors of the league, much to the delight of long-disheartened New York fans.

The 1968–69 race in the Eastern Division was thus the most exciting in years. Two establishment teams, Boston and Philadelphia, were being chal-

GOING UP FOR A REBOUND AGAINST CAZZIE RUSSELL OF THE NEW YORK KNICKERBOCKERS.

lenged by a pair of upstarts, Baltimore and New York, in a tight championship scramble; and competition among these four teams was intense all season long.

The Bullets won their season's opener against the Detroit Pistons, 124–116, on October 16, with Earl scoring twenty-eight points. After a close loss to the 76'ers, Baltimore won three and lost two, then went on a winning streak of six straight that pushed them past Boston into first place in the Eastern Division, unfamiliar surroundings indeed for the Bullets. Over these first thirteen games Earl led the league in scoring with twenty-eight points a game, and he ranked fourth in assists, 7.4 per game.

Boston and Baltimore continued to struggle over the divisional lead during the early weeks of the season; and on December first the Bullets had a slim game-and-a-half lead over the Celtics, with the 76'ers in third place. Eight games off the pace, way back in sixth, were the then under-achieving Knicks. Earl was now fourth in league scoring, 25.9 points per game, and fifth in assists, 6.4 per game.

A week later Boston had tied the Bullets for first, but the Baltimore record stood at twenty games won and seven lost. Two years before twenty victories had been an entire season's worth of Bullet wins, and here they had won that many by early December. The rest of the league began to talk less of "early-season flash" and take the Bullets a little more seriously.

Playing a fast-breaking firehouse style of basketball, the Bullets ran off a string of nine straight victories that concluded with a win over Seattle on Christmas Day. Thanks in large measure to Earl's scoring and playmaking as well as Wes Unseld's rebounding, the Bullets were now three and a half games ahead of Philadelphia, Boston having dropped to third.

Just before Christmas, however, Detroit and New York made the trade that would eventually have great influence on Bullet fortunes. Forward Dave DeBusschere came to New York and Willis Reed was moved back into the pivot for the Knicks, a combination that turned New York into a winning ballclub (eight in a row and fourteen out of fifteen after the trade) and started them on their way to the playoffs.

At All-Star time in January, Baltimore still had a three-game lead over Philadelphia, a margin of three and a half over Boston, and five games over New York. Earl was then averaging twenty-five points a game, fourth highest in the league, and his 5.8 assists per game had slipped to seventh best in the NBA.

KNICKS WILLIS REED AND CAZZIE RUSSELL BLOCK A MONROE DRIVE, DECEMBER 31, 1968.

Three Bullets, the maximum number of All-Stars allowed from any one team, had been selected to play for the East. In addition to the trio of Earl, forward Gus Johnson and center Wes Unseld, Gene Shue was coaching the East; and the game was held in Baltimore as well. The local fans took advantage of the chance to see their stars play against the best in the league, and every seat in Civic Center was taken that night.

The Bullet-dominated East had been heavily favored before the game, but their lead at halftime was only 60–53. The West trailed by a mere three points at the end of the third quarter, and with eight minutes left in the game the West upset the predictions by going ahead, 96–94.

Cincinnati guard Oscar Robertson, the greatest all-round player in the NBA and the accepted standard of excellence for professional basketball, rallied with two three-point plays to bring the East back, 101–96. It was then that Bullet fans had their biggest chance of the evening to cheer as local heroes Earl and Gus Johnson combined to score eleven points for the East, one basket coming after a spectacular pass from Earl to Gus the full length of the court. These eleven points eventually proved the margin of victory as the East won, 123–112.

Oscar Robertson was named Most Valuable Player of the event. Oscar was competing in his ninth straight All-Star Game and Earl was playing his first, and Earl played five minutes less than

Oscar. Still, it was an unusual opportunity to compare their performances against the same team on the same night.

Earl was second to Oscar in points scored (twenty-one to twenty-four), made one less assist (four as against five), and had two fewer rebounds (four instead of six). Oscar's shooting percentage

SEATTLE'S LEN WILKENS GUARDS EARL DURING THE 1969 NBA ALL-STAR GAME.

was .500 as compared to Earl's .400; and Earl went nine for twelve at the free-throw line, whereas Oscar swished eight of eight. While statistical differences are not always important, and Earl was, after all, only an NBA sophomore, most observers agree that he is not yet in Oscar's class, particularly as a playmaker. But then, no one else is either; and many experts do think that of all the younger NBA guards, Earl is the most likely to eventually equal the Big O.

Near the end of January, Earl's average tailed off to 24.6 points a game, and he was no longer within the top eight NBA players in assists. Then, on February 5, in an even more serious development for the Bullets, All-Star forward Gus Johnson injured his left knee in a game against the Celtics. Earl and Kevin Loughery, the Bullets' other starting guard, staged a fourth-quarter rally to save the game for Baltimore, but Johnson was lost to the team for the rest of the season.

Fortunately the Bullet bench was strong and versatile, and Earl and Kevin Loughery were able to maintain their high-scoring ways. A week later, trailing Chicago 92–90 in the fourth quarter with nine minutes to go, Earl scored ten of his then game-high thirty-three points. This led Baltimore to a

124–116 victory that increased the Bullet lead over the second-place club to three games. But that second-place team was no longer Boston or Philadelphia—it was the vastly improved New York Knicks, now playing some of the best ball in the league.

The 76'ers managed to overtake New York for second place in the weeks that followed, but the Celtics remained an unaccustomed fourth, nine games out. Meanwhile, Earl was high scorer for the Bullets in game after game boosting his average to 25.7, second best in the league; and Baltimore maintained its first-place position.

In the middle of March Baltimore played New York in a game so closely fought that the score was tied eleven times and there were twelve changes of lead. Baltimore won by the slimmest of margins, 111–110; and the rivalry intensified further when the two teams met again a week later. The Knicks were still fighting with Philadelphia for second place, while a victory for the Bullets that night would clinch their first Eastern title. Baltimore led at the half, 50–44, but when the Knick defense tightened, New York surged ahead, only to have the Bullets come back in the fourth quarter, 79–77. In spite of some fine outside shooting by Earl, the

Knicks outscored the Bullets in the final few minutes and won the critical contest, 104-100.

Two nights later Earl poured in forty-one points as the Bullets broke a halftime tie to defeat the Chicago Bulls, 115-103, and establish themselves champions of the Eastern Division at last. The team held an uproarious champagne party in Chicago following their victory, and the fans back in Baltimore had noisy celebrations of their own; for the Bullets had not only gone from last to first, they had done it in a single season.

But the annual NBA playoffs have often been called a "second season" because of their lengthy schedule and intense competition. And as division champions the Bullets' first 1969 playoff opponent was the East's third-place team, the New York Knicks.

Earl was troubled by his arthritic knees, yet he scored thirty-two points in the first playoff game of his career and was also high man for both teams in the second. As a club, however, the Bullets were quickly subdued by the smooth team-play of the Knicks. In a surprising upset they lost four straight games to New York and were swiftly eliminated from the playoffs. Considering the Bullets' great improvement during the regular schedule, the second season was a short and disappointing one in Baltimore.

5
PLAYOFF UPSET

WHEN THE NBA campaign of 1969–70 got under way, the fans soon became aware of important changes that had taken place within the Eastern Division since the preceding year. The formerly mighty Boston Celtics, winners of their eleventh NBA championship the past spring, were now rebuilding and no longer contenders, for one thing. Rookie center Lew Alcindor of the Milwaukee Bucks was proving as good as his publicity for another, taking the Bucks all the way to the playoffs in only their second season, after a last-place finish in their first.

Dominating the division all season long, however, were the New York Knicks. Employing the same mobile team-offense and strong pressing defense that had upset the Bullets in the 1969 playoffs, the Knicks lost only one of their first twenty-four games, winning eighteen of them in a row for an NBA record. At the end of the first month of the schedule New York was already six games in front of second-place Baltimore and was not to be challenged for the rest of the year.

By the All-Star break in January, Alcindor and the Bucks had surged past Baltimore, dropping the Bullets to third place; but the Knicks remained solidly in first. New York continued to hold a wide advantage throughout the second half of the season, finishing the eighty-two games of the regular schedule four games ahead of Milwaukee and ten games in front of Baltimore. As first- and third-place finishers in the East in 1970, New York and Baltimore then continued their playoff rivalry by again meeting in the first round.

Of the six games between the Knicks and the Bullets during the regular season, Baltimore had been able to win only one. Counting the four straight playoff losses at the end of the previous season, Baltimore went into the 1970 playoffs with a feeble one-and-nine record against New York. But the Bullets had a marked change of form during post-season play once again; and this time it was for the better.

Baltimore spurted away to a fast ten-point lead

in the opening game; but the Knick offense soon sharpened, and a tight, exciting battle followed with neither team able to hold the lead for long. New York eventually pushed to a six-point lead halfway through the fourth quarter, holding the margin until Earl's graceful fallaway jumper brought the score to 94–90 with six minutes left. After successive baskets by Wes Unseld and Gus Johnson had tied for the Bullets, Earl put Baltimore ahead at 96–94; and when New York rallied to tie the score twice more, his sharpshooting broke the tie each time.

With only twenty-seven seconds remaining and the Bullets leading by two points, the Knicks' Bill Bradley sank a clutch basket that tied the game at 102. Baltimore then held the ball for the last shot, only to have Earl's try hit the rim a second before the end of regulation play and leave the score still tied.

The Bullets were able to score first in the five-minute overtime period that followed and maintain the slim lead until the forty-five-second mark. At that point Dick Barnett of New York stole the ball, was fouled, and sank both free throws to once more tie the score, 110–110. Again Baltimore held for the last shot; but as Earl was dribbling to use up time the quick hands of Walt Frazier tapped the ball to Dick Barnett who drove for a layup. When he missed

EARL PASSES OFF AGAINST NEW YORK. THE KNICKS ARE GUARD WALT FRAZIER AND CENTER WILLIS REED.

his shot at the buzzer, the game was sent into double overtime; and the fans in Madison Square Garden edged even further forward in their seats.

New York pulled away to a five-point lead in the second overtime; Baltimore then fought back and tied the score, 117–117, with only forty-three seconds to go. The Knicks finally prevailed, however, when a basket by Willis Reed and a free throw by Dave DeBusschere in the closing moments gave them a 120–117 victory.

Nevertheless, Earl was the high scorer for both teams with thirty-nine points; and the Bullets had played their best game of the season, particularly on defense. Encouraged, they did equally well in the second game of the 1970 playoffs and stayed in front of the Knicks until the fourth quarter. New York then scrambled to a seven-point lead, sparked by the aggressive play of sub Mike Riordan, and went on to win its sixth playoff game in a row from Baltimore, 106–99.

Earl totaled twenty-five points, again the high man for both clubs, as the Bullets mounted an even stronger offense in the third game. Center Wes Unseld grabbed thirty-four rebounds, more than the team total for New York; and the combination enabled a jubilant Baltimore team to win its first playoff victory in five years, 127–113.

Underdog Baltimore also won the fourth game, with Earl contributing thirty-four points to a 102–92 effort that evened the series at two games for each club. The Bullet offense sagged in the fifth contest (New York 101, Baltimore 80); but in the sixth meeting Gus Johnson had thiry-one points and Earl hit for twenty-nine. This gave the Bullets a 96–87 win, nearly raised the roof of Baltimore's Civic Auditorium, and extended the series to a showdown seventh game.

The decisive encounter of the 1970 New York-Baltimore playoffs began as another close struggle.

DAVE DEBUSSCHERE OF THE KNICKS TRIES TO STOP ONE OF EARL'S ACROBATIC SHOTS.

The Bullets gradually began to make more mistakes than the Knicks, however, turning the ball over more often; and they got into early foul trouble as well. Ahead by only five points at the end of the first quarter, the Knicks led 62–47 at the half.

Earl was again the outstanding offensive player on both teams (thirty-two points overall); but the balanced team-play of the Knicks proved more effective, and New York defeated Baltimore, 127–114. The loss concluded the year for a disappointed Baltimore team, while New York went on to crush Milwaukee in the East and then defeat Los Angeles, finalists in the Western Division, to become the 1970 champions of the NBA.

The rapidly increasing popularity of basketball led to further league expansion the following season in which four realigned divisions replaced the former two. New York remained with the tough eastern teams in the Atlantic Division; and Baltimore was placed in the Central Division where the competition turned out to be much easier.

Both New York and Baltimore took first place in their divisions during 1970–1971 with little trouble. The Knicks seemed to have lost some of their edge, however, not playing as consistently as they had in their championship season. And even the Bullets' own fans did not take their division lead entirely seriously because the other teams in their division had such a poor record.

Meanwhile the Milwaukee Bucks of the Midwest Division in the Western Conference became the top club of the league. Not only were they paced by the overwhelming seven-foot, three-inch Lew Alcindor at center, they had been further strengthened by trading for a second superstar, the great Oscar Robertson of Cincinnati. In only their third season in the NBA, the Bucks won every game on their exhibition schedule, broke the Knicks' record of the previous year by winning twenty games in a row during the regular season, and finished with a 66-and-16 record, second-best in the history of the league.

In spite of the Bucks' runaway superiority over the rest of the NBA during 1970–1971, one team did manage to contain them. The defending champion New York Knicks beat Milwaukee four of the five times they met, and most fans expected the two clubs to eventually clash in a historic playoff series for the 1971 championship.

There were the semifinals to be played first, however. While the Knicks and Bucks had an easy time of it against Atlanta and San Francisco, Baltimore's first-round opponent was the scrappy Philadelphia

76'ers. Considering the Bullets' .512 won-lost record during the regular season, only ninth best in the league, the press was not optimistic about their chances.

Baltimore's extensive injury list was another serious disadvantage. Wes Unseld was recovering from a badly sprained ankle, Gus Johnson had not been playing much because of two bad knees, Kevin Loughery was suffering from a sore heel, and Eddie Miles had one leg in a cast.

To make matters worse, someone accidentally jammed a knee into Earl's ribs during the opener against Philadelphia, and he had to leave the game. Baltimore lost without him (126–112); but won the second game (119–107) when he scored twenty-four points in spite of needing three injections of a painkiller.

During the first half of the third game a stray elbow dug into Earl's injured ribs, causing him so much pain that he went into shock and could not even remember his name. Nevertheless, padded with foam-rubber and shooting with his usual acrobatic flair, he came back in the second half to score twenty-three points in the last twenty-four minutes; and the Bullets defeated Philadelphia, 111–103.

The Bullets also took the fourth contest of the

bruising series, only to drop the fifth and sixth games to the battling 76'ers. Then, breaking the deciding seventh game wide open in the second quarter, they finally eliminated Philadelphia, 128–120, and thereby qualified to meet their old rivals, the Knicks.

New York had an injury problem of its own that season, an old knee ailment of center Willis Reed's having flared up; and during the Bullet series his recently sprained right shoulder was to increase New York's difficulties. Still, the Bullets being the Bullets and barely able to floor five healthy starters in the bargain, the experts predicted a relatively easy series for the Knicks and continued to look ahead to a big Milwaukee–New York final.

The Knicks did win the opening game, a 112–111 squeaker, as well as the second, 107–88. But the supposedly overmatched Bullets snapped back to trounce New York in the next two games, 114–88 and 101–80, surprising nearly everyone with their effective team offense and very tough defense. The faltering Knicks gained a one-game advantage with a slim 89–84 victory in the fifth meeting; and Baltimore came back to take the sixth, 113–96, reducing the series to a final seventh game.

In the first six games Earl's spectacular shooting made him the high-point man three times and second-highest once, his only "off night" coming in the second game when he sprained an ankle. He also tied Dick Barnett of the Knicks for most scoring in the seventh game; and the rest of the exciting climax was almost as close.

New York led by two at the end of the first quarter, and by four at the half. Baltimore, in turn, held a five-point lead at the end of the third quarter; then, with less than three minutes left, New York went ahead again, 88–87. Earl quickly put the Bullets back in front, 89–88; and Baltimore clung to a slender lead as the game—and the series—came to a close.

With the score 93–91, only seconds left, and elimination at hand, New York came streaking downcourt, desperately trying for a tie. Bill Bradley took the last shot from the corner where he is usually extremely accurate, but Wes Unseld sprung high to block it as the game ended; and Baltimore had at last defeated New York in the playoffs with a brilliant upset.

And so it was the Bullets, not the Knicks, who met Milwaukee in the NBA finals for 1971. Tired and hurting, the Baltimore team was no match for the seemingly invincible Bucks, however. Milwaukee, having already breezed past San Francisco and Los Angeles, swept the Bullets in four straight games to compile the best playoff record ever for an NBA champion, twelve games won and only two lost.

Although there was immediately much talk about a new basketball dynasty having been founded in Milwaukee, Baltimore fans took some consolation in remembering. After all, the same thing had been said about the Knicks only the year before, and look what the Bullets had done to them.

6
"BEST IN THE WORLD?"

FLASHY in his actions on the floor, Earl is deceptively mild in appearance, although he does admit to a quick temper. He has worn a dapper mustache since his Winston-Salem days; his hair is cut in a restrained Afro style, and his general manner is smoothly quiet. Besides his usual number ten, he is most easily recognized when at rest on the court by the sweatband that is generally on his right wrist.

It is problems with his knees that have become as characteristic of Earl as his showy style of play, however. Partially the result of all those hours pounding up and down macadam playground courts as a boy, Earl's knees have been inflamed with arthritis; and he has suffered from bursitis in them as well.

EARL DEMONSTRATES HIS FORM AT THE FREE-THROW LINE.

These are the same conditions that have affected Joe Namath, and Earl's knees are just as critical to his future and that of his team as Joe's are. They have also received nearly as much publicity, particularly when they were operated upon in the summer of 1970.

"I got to get it all as soon as I can," Earl was once quoted as saying in reference to his physical condition, explaining on another occasion, "Money is what the thing is all about."

Single and still a resident of Philadelphia, he has had much respect for the guidance and help of his mother and older sister, particularly during the time he was in college; and he recently purchased a new home for his family in Philadelphia. Earl is also a devoted admirer of the late Dr. Martin Luther King, Jr., and wore a black mourning-patch on the left shoulder of his basketball jersey throughout the 1968–1969 season.

He has worked for Rev. Leon Sullivan's Opportunities Industrialization Center in Philadelphia during his offseason. The Center has had considerable success in training ghetto Negroes in vocational skills and then locating jobs for them; and Earl has expressed great interest in this and similar community action programs. An elementary education major at Winston-Salem, three times on the Dean's List, he also enjoys working with street-based youth programs. From his own experience, he strongly advocates that disadvantaged youth stay in school rather than drop out.

On his day off, he has been quoted as saying, he

TWISTING AND LEAPING HIGH, EARL GETS OFF ONE OF HIS SPECTACULAR ONE-HANDED SHOTS.

stretches on the bed, eats potato chips, and watches television. He is also a constant listener to comedy records, favoring Bill Cosby, who comes from the same neighborhood in Philadelphia. Another of his spare-time activities is magic, and Earl has performed his sleight-of-hand routine during the half-time of Bullet games.

As for his future, assuming that Earl's brittle knees hold up he seems destined to continue as one of the NBA's superstars for some time. His season's scoring average dropped to 21.4 in 1971 from its high of 25.8 in 1969, it is true; and he was fourteenth in the NBA for scoring in 1971 as compared to second in 1969. But his defensive skills and team-play have improved over the same period; he now seems somewhat more durable than before his knee operation; and his unique offensive moves frustrate the rest of the league more than ever.

In any case, the excitement that Earl generates as he streaks loosely downcourt, head wagging and knees wobbling ("I don't know what I'm going to do with the ball, and if I don't know, I'm quite sure the guy guarding me doesn't know, either"), cannot be measured in numbers. When he goes up for one of his self-styled "flukey-dukey" shots, his fans happily shout, "Earl, Earl, Best in the World," and if his defense is not always up to the same level, he remains the most exciting one-on-one offensive player in the game.